doll Travel

Trips to take and crafts to make!

American Girl®

Published by American Girl Publishing
Copyright © 2013, 2015 American Girl

Questions or comments? Call 1-800-845-0005,
visit **americangirl.com,** or write to
Customer Service, American Girl,
8400 Fairway Place, Middleton, WI 53562-0497.

Printed in China
16 17 18 19 20 21 22 23 24 LEO 10 9 8 7 6 5 4 3 2

Editorial Development: Trula Magruder

Art Direction & Design: Gretchen Becker, Camela Decaire,
Sigrid Hubertz

Production: Jeannette Bailey, Sarah Boecher,
Judith Lary, Tami Kepler, Jolene Schulz, Kristi Tabrizi

Illustration: Casey Lukatz

Stylists: Meghan Hurley, Casey Hull, Trula Magruder

Doll Stylist: Kim Sphar

Cover Photography: Joe Hinrichs, Stephen Rebout

Tabletop Photography: Kristin Kurt

Special thanks to hand model Kerry G.

Photography & illustrations for kit supplies: Ng Maps/
National Geographic Stock (maps); © iStockphoto/mart_m
(mobile phone); © iStockphoto/nwinter (bank cards);
© iStockphoto/mamado (fish); © iStockphoto/daveporter
(dollars); © iStockphoto/anzlyldrm (MP3 player); © iStock-
photo/kysa (GPS picture); © iStockphoto/JamesGdesign
(tags & labels); © iStockphoto/kathykonkle (travel stickers);
© iStockphoto/ctoelg (Euros); © iStockphoto/-A3K- (world
flags); © iStockphoto/dee-jay (skier on pass); © iStock-
photo/garywg (cruise ship); © iStockphoto/ma_rish (Italy);
© iStockphoto/erakula (European cities); © iStockphoto/
Axusha (Australian patterns); © iStockphoto/DrawnToBeWild
(Eiffel Tower); © iStockphoto/Tomacco (British royal
guard); © iStockphoto/Talshiar (GPS); © iStockphoto/
RUSSELLTATEdotCOM (clock, vacation icons, British coins).

Dear Doll Lover,

What's your dream vacation? A thrilling theme-park trip? A lazy day on a sandy beach? A sunny tropical cruise? You can imagine your ideal outing by creating doll-sized trips using the ideas inside this book. You'll also find a real duffel bag, a passport, international maps, airline tickets, souvenirs, doll money, and more. It's everything you need to create a one-of-a-kind experience for your doll—and yourself.

You also can find loads of ideas for taking your doll along on real family vacations. Learn what to pack and how to take travel pics like a pro. And you'll discover tricks to keep your doll safe on all her journeys.

Are you there yet?

Your friends at American Girl

Craft with Care

Keep Your Doll Safe

When creating doll crafts, remember that dyes from ribbons, felt, beads, cords, fabrics, fleece, and other supplies may bleed onto your doll or her clothes and leave permanent stains. To help prevent this, use lighter colors when possible, and check your doll often to make sure the colors aren't transferring to her body, her vinyl, or her clothes. And never get your doll wet! Water and heat greatly increase dye rub-off.

It's Just Pretend

All the doll crafts in this book are for pretend only. So don't wet your doll's craft-foam soap, leave her camping gear out in the rain, or expose her to too much sand, sun, or snow.

Get Help!

When you see this symbol 🖐 in the book, it means that you need an adult to help you with all or a part of the craft. ALWAYS ask for help before continuing.

Ask First

If a craft asks you to reuse an old item, such as a magazine or a piece of clothing, always ask an adult for permission before you use it. Your parent might still need it, so check first.

Craft Smart

If a craft instruction says "cut," use scissors. If it says "glue," use craft glue or adhesive dots. And if it says "paint," use a nontoxic acrylic paint. Before you use these supplies, ask an adult to check them over— especially the paints and glues. Some crafting supplies are not safe for kids.

Put Away Crafts and Supplies

When you're not using the crafts or craft supplies, put them up high or store them away from little kids and pets. Toddlers and animals might eat your crafts, break them, or even hurt themselves when playing with them.

Search for Supplies

If you can't find an unusual or seasonal craft item, such as plastic paper or fabric treat bags, at your local stores, ask an adult to check at scrapbook or craft stores or to search online. You can also see if a local store can order the supplies.

GLUE

Ski Resort

Send your doll swooshing through the snow on skis or a snowboard.

Snow Skis & Poles

Send your doll down the ski slopes in style! To make each ski, attach plastic paper to sticky craft foam. Trace the kit's ski pattern onto the foam, and cut out the ski. Ask an adult to replace the metal from a clothespin with a rubber band. Attach the clothespin to the ski with adhesive dots as shown on the pattern. For each pole, wrap a 10- or 12-inch-long dowel in silver duct tape, twisting the tape just beyond the bottom. Punch a hole in the center of a craft foam circle, and slip it on near the bottom of the dowel. Tape a ribbon loop on the top of the pole for your doll's wrist.

Snowboard & Pass

Strap your doll's feet to this fun snowboard! Attach plastic paper to sticky craft foam. Trace the kit's snowboard pattern onto the foam, and cut it out. Punch four holes in the board as shown on the pattern. Slip two 8-inch ribbons through the holes as shown to make loops on the plastic side. Tape the ribbon ends flat to the foam side.

Give your doll access to the slopes with the kit's ski pass. Ask an adult to use a mini safety pin to attach the pass to your doll's coat zipper or jacket pocket.

Winter Park

Bundle up your doll for a day
of ice-skating and snowshoeing.

Ice Skates

If your doll doesn't already
own skates, make a pair! Attach
mini clothespins to the center
of your doll's boot soles with
adhesive dots. If you like, ask an
adult to paint the clothespins
silver. Let the paint dry completely.

Snowshoes

1. For a snowshoe frame, cut and connect 8 bendy straws, following the kit's snowshoe pattern. Wrap each connection with colored duct tape.

2. Attach plastic paper to sticky craft foam. Press adhesive dots around the bottom of the frame, press it to the plastic, and trim around the frame.

3. Lift the frame to punch holes (see the pattern). Pull the ends of an 18-inch ribbon up through the holes, and crisscross the ribbon over your doll's boots. Tie in back.

Sandy Beach

Take your doll to a tropical paradise for a little fun in the sun.

Beach Gear

Give your doll great gear for a tropical getaway. For a beach umbrella, open a compact umbrella. Spread out a hand towel for a beach towel. For sunscreen, slip craft paper inside an empty plastic tube, and attach the kit's sunscreen label. Pull out the kit's magazine, and assemble it following the instructions. For a cute beach bag, flip the umbrella's fabric case inside out, fold up the long bottom and tape it to one side, and then turn the bag right-side out again.

Bodyboard

Let your doll show off her surfing moves with a body-board. To make one, attach **plastic paper** to **sticky craft foam**. Trace the **kit's board pattern** onto the foam, and cut it out. **Punch** a hole in the board (see the pattern). Slip in an 8-inch **ribbon,** knot it in back, and make a wrist loop in front with an **adhesive dot.**

Ice Chest & Sodas

Chill your doll's drinks in a cooler. To make it, cover a small craft box with colored duct tape. Use adhesive dots to attach mini clothespins to the sides for handles. Add the kit's cooler label. For permanent ice, fill the box with clear beads, squeeze in glue, and let dry. For sodas, cover small thread spools with colored duct tape, glue paper circles to each end, and add the kit's soda labels.

11

Cruise Ship

Book your doll on a boat for a little R & R.

Tropical Drinks

Serve deck-side sippers. For each drink, coat the inside of a plastic cap with acrylic paint, and pour out extra paint. Let dry. Cut a slit in a craft-foam circle, and slip the foam onto the cap's edge. Drop in a stem of flowers and a mini straw.

Sweet Sundress

⭐ Ask an adult if you can cut a long sleeve off an old T-shirt. For each armhole, cut a 1-inch slit 1½ inches from the hemmed edge. Cut the dress to any length, and if you like, hem with adhesive dots. You can add an appliqué, a ribbon belt, or ribbon trim.

Sea Pass Card

Slip a thin ribbon through the kit's sea pass, and tie the ribbon around your doll's neck.

Cruise Shoes

✋ For darling deck sandals, attach plastic paper to sticky craft foam. Trace the kit's shoe pattern twice onto the foam, flip the pattern, and trace it 2 more times. Cut out all 4 soles. Ask an adult to trim two 3-inch cuffs off an old sock, and hem the long sides with adhesive dots. For each shoe, tape the ends of a sock to the bottom edges of a foam sole near the toe. Then stick the second sole over the first one. Add an appliqué where shown.

Fishing & Hiking

Your doll will love a nature vacation filled with fun hikes and fish stories.

GPS

Help your doll track her location with the kit's handheld GPS.

Backpack

Offer your doll a hiking pack to haul her gear. To make it, attach 2 ribbon straps to the back of a fabric treat bag with adhesive dots. To decorate, use the dots to attach ribbon loops, and then weave a cord through the loops as shown. Slip the cord ends through a bead.

Canteen

Your doll will need a water flask when she hits the trail. To make one, use a wood disk or button for the canteen. Attach a pony bead to the top and a ribbon strap to each back edge with adhesive dots. Press on the kit's canteen label.

Fishing Pole

Make your doll a lightweight rod that's easy to tote. To make it, pull out the kit's fish, and attach it to a string with a mini adhesive dot. Tie the string at the top of a thin dowel. Slip a clear rubber band around your doll's hands so that she can hold the pole.

15

Amusement Park

Ready your doll for rides and attractions at a theme park.

Day Pack

Your doll can tote a small bag to keep her supplies handy. To make it, ask an adult if you can trim the top corner off an old nylon drawstring bag. Seal the cut edges with adhesive dots. Fold colored duct tape into two narrow straps, and attach the straps to the back edges of the bag with adhesive dots. If you like, add a new drawstring and an appliqué.

Park Provisions

Bring a water bottle for your doll to carry around. To make one, attach the kit's water label to an empty mini plastic bottle. For park admission, use an adhesive dot to fasten one of the kit's wristbands around your doll's wrist.

Ice Cream Cone

Treat your doll to something sweet. Roll the kit's waffle cone into a cone shape, and seal it with adhesive dots. Glue 2 white pom-poms together for a double dip of vanilla ice cream, and then run glue around the inside rim and slip in the scoops.

Big City

Dress your doll in glamour and glitz for an evening out on the town.

Evening Gowns

Slip your doll into a dazzling dress. To make one, ask an adult if you can cut the leg off an old pair of **shiny leggings**. For each armhole, cut a 1-inch slit 1½ inches from the hemmed edge. Gently slip the dress onto your doll, leaving the length extra long. Pull out your doll's fancy gloves if she has a pair.

Caution: Not all fabrics are the same. If you use a darker color, review page 4. Then check your doll often to make sure the fabric dye hasn't rubbed off onto your doll!

Show Tickets

Don't forget to pick up the **kit's Broadway tickets** for an evening of spectacular entertainment.

Brilliant Bling

Dress your doll in big-city sparklers. For a choker, use an **adhesive dot** to secure a **metallic ribbon** around your doll's neck. For a pearl bracelet, string **white pearl beads** onto an **elastic cord**. For a ruby ring, slip a **red bead** onto an elastic cord, tying the knot as close to the bead as you can. Use **adhesive gems** for diamond earrings.

Faux Mink Stole

Drape your doll in a fancy fur. Cut a 7-by-13-inch piece of **craft fur**. Rub the cut piece over the garbage to remove loose fibers. Slip the wrap around your doll's shoulders, and hold it closed with a **sparkling pin**.

Vacation Gear

Don't forget these items when traveling by land, air, or sea.

Electronics

Bring the kit's camera for vacation pics. Attach each end of a ribbon strap to the back of the camera with adhesive dots. Bring the kit's cell phone to check flights. Attach the kit's MP3 player to sticky craft foam, and trim around the player. Tie a bead to each end of a cord, and tape the cord to the back of the player for headphones.

Travel Pillow

Pull out the pillow pattern, and trace it twice on fleece. Cut out the fleece, and glue the edges together, leaving one end opened. Let dry. Stuff the pillow with fiberfill. Use a dowel to push the filling all the way to the end, and then glue the seams closed. (If needed, use binder clips to hold the edges until the glue dries.)

Currency & Documents

Before your doll takes off on any international trips, give her the kit's money, debit card, airline ticket, metro travel pass, and passport.

Hotel Essentials

Don't forget these small comforts to help make a hotel a home.

Travel Clock

Your doll can back up the hotel's clock with her own travel clock. To make it, pull out the kit's travel clock face and clock stand. Fold the stand, and tape it to the back of the clock so that the clock stands upright.

Toiletries

★ Pack travel-sized toiletries for the trip. Ask an adult if you can cut a square corner off an old washcloth. For a toothbrush, use adhesive dots to attach a white tube bead to a flattened piece of drinking straw. For a bar of soap, glue together 2 white craft foam rectangles.

Slippers

Your doll will love these fluffy slippers after hours of touring. Follow the "cruise shoes" instructions on page 13, but use a single sole, and instead of a sock strap, cut a 3-by-1-inch craft-fur strap. Attach the strap, and then trim the fur on the bottom down to the fabric lining so that the slipper sole rests flat on the floor.

Travel Totes

Your doll will travel in style with these bags and baggage.

Toiletries Bag

Keep your doll's toiletries in their own separate bag. (Avoid any liquids if she's flying!) Ask an adult if you can cut a rectangle section off the corner of an old vinyl bag, keeping the zipper and zipper pull. Cover the zipper's cut end with clear tape, and seal the 2 cut seams with adhesive dots.

Carry-on Case

An aluminum suitcase will protect your doll's belongings from the bumps and bustle of travel. To make one, decorate a metal craft tin with strips of colored duct tape. Use adhesive dots to attach a wide colored craft stick to the back edge of the tin, a ribbon loop to the other end of the stick, and beads to the bottom of the tin for wheels. If you like, personalize the case with the kit's luggage labels and luggage tag.

Duffel Bag

Fill the kit's duffel bag with any
in-flight accessories your doll might
like, such as the kit's deck of playing
cards for a game of solitaire or the
kit's city maps to study the streets
of Paris and London before landing.

Souvenir Shop

Bring home mini mementos of your doll's journeys.

Paintings

Create mini masterpieces for your doll to buy from street vendors. Paint impressionist-style art on tiny canvases.

Flag Magnets

Make magnets of world flags for your doll to collect on her travels. Attach an adhesive magnetic strip to the back of your kit's flag art, and trim around the designs.

Prints and Postcards

Pretend to mail the kit's postcards to your doll's loved ones, but keep the kit's travel posters as souvenirs.

©/TM 2012 American Girl

T-Shirts

Make souvenir tees for your doll to purchase in shops. To make them, attach stickers, appliqués, and adhesive letters to doll-sized T-shirts.

New York

$3.95

.95
3.00

SEASHELLS by the SEASHORE

Travel Tips

Real doll travel demands that you plan ahead!

Don't Overpack

Bring a few pairs of shoes, pj's, a dress for special occasions, and play clothes for your doll. Add a swimsuit for summer or a coat for winter. That's it!

Organize Small Stuff

Slip small items—such as shoes, socks, or hair accessories—into clear resealable bags. That way, you'll be able to peek into a bag to quickly find what your doll needs.

Take a Tote

You may need to take stairs, carry your own travel gear, or even rush to catch a flight, so carry your doll in a backpack or tote to keep your hands free.

Remember Your Doll

If you tell your doll your plans every step of the way, you'll keep better track of her. Say "Jen, we're boarding a plane now, so don't be scared," and you'll know that Jen's not sitting in the airport's waiting area. Also, place her where you can see her at all times. If you're in a hotel, keep your doll on a counter or near your bag so that you'll spot her before checking out.

Make Memories

Include your doll in real vacation snapshots. Pose her with you or family members so that your doll will have mementos of her travels.

Super Snapshots

Use these simple photo tricks to create your doll's vacation pics.

Snap Fast for Safety

Your doll should avoid too much sun, sand, heat, water, and snow. So after taking photos, bring your doll back inside to protect her from the elements.

Add Details

Choose a vacation location, and then add scenic props, such as shells or a small pail.

Size Scenery

Human-sized trees, soda cans, and footprints will look odd in your doll's photos, so erase signs of the "big world" and surround your doll with stuff that suits her size.

Make It Real

Pose your doll to bring her pictures to life! Turn her head to chat with friends, move her arms to wave, or sit her up to get a better view—just as you and your friends might do!

Out and About

Invite your doll along on family outings.

Try these mini vacations:

Visit relatives.

Dine at a restaurant patio.

Dress up and take family photos.

Feed ducks at a pond.

Ride on a bike path.

Pick wildflowers.

Attend an outdoor concert.

Go to the zoo.

Search for shapes in the clouds.

Walk through a corn maze.

See a movie.

Take a trip to the mailbox,
and let us know what
kind of vacations
you give your doll!

Write to
Doll Travel Editor
American Girl
8400 Fairway Place
Middleton, WI 53562

(Sorry, but photos can't be returned. All comments
and suggestions received by American Girl may be
used without compensation or acknowledgment.)

Here are some other American Girl books you might like:

Doll School

Doll Hair Salon

Doll Tees Felt Fashions

Doll Dining

Doll Pets

play@
☆ American Girl™

Discover online games, quizzes, activities,
and more at **americangirl.com**